The Money 20

The Money 20

What 20-Somethings Want to Know About Money

Linda Schoenfeld, CFP®

This publication contains the opinions and ideas of the author. While she has used her best efforts in writing this book, she cannot guarantee the accuracy of the contents. Please refer to the Resources page at the end of the book, where the reader will find the most up to date information at all the referenced web sites.

Copyediting by EbookEditingServices.com

Cover Design by DigitalDonna.com

Cartoons by Glasbergen Cartoon Service

Copyright © 2015 Linda Schoenfeld, CFP*

ISBN-13: 9781518879647
ISBN-10: 1518879640

TABLE OF
CONTENTS

INTRODUCTION

Most personal finance books are very detailed and overwhelm you with information. This book is different. It is short and sweet. It is in a question and answer format, making it easy to read and understand. You can skip around, focusing on your concerns, or read it from beginning to end. Most of the questions are taken from my 20-something son and daughter, and their friends. Other questions are the ones that were asked most often in the hundreds of money management workshops I taught over the years. Many of the individuals I taught were baby boomers, with well-established financial habits. So many of my students were frustrated that they had never been taught the basics of money management. How they wished they would have known what is in this book when they were in their twenties!

The twenties are an exciting and challenging time. You are on your own financially, and the decisions you make, and the habits you develop, will set your financial course for decades to come. If you can build a strong financial foundation now, it will pay dividends for the rest of your life.

The first step in building that foundation is to learn the language of money. Unfortunately, through all of your years of schooling, the language of money and personal money management was probably not taught, so you are on your own with this education. Read a few personal finance books, do some online research, and ask questions when you don't understand something. You may have spent four or more years learning and figuring out HOW you were going to make money. Now it is time to learn how to manage the millions of dollars you will be making over your working life. And yes, if you do the math, it will be millions!

The next step in building your strong financial foundation is to develop good money habits. These habits include spending less than you earn, minimizing and paying off debt, paying your bills on time, developing a spending plan, and saving for the future. Pretty basic stuff.

Money management is an art, not a science. There are many different ways to get to the same goal. Take what you can from each book that you read. As every situation is different, some advice will be good for you right now, and some advice might not fit your circumstances. Some aspects of money management are non-negotiable, such as spending less than you earn and paying off debt as quickly as possible. Other advice, such as signing up for your company 401(k) plan, although good, might not be right for you at this stage of your life.

The average American has a very low savings rate, is saddled with credit card debt, has a hefty car payment, and possibly a mortgage payment that is way too high. The average American is only two paychecks away from financial difficulty, and that cuts across most income levels.

Don't be average! You can do better. If you start out with good financial habits, you won't get to your forties or fifties and ask, "What the hell happened?"

My hope for you, is that I will not see you in one of my workshops when you are middle-aged. I hope you will be money smart, pay off your debts, and develop good financial habits. I hope you are wildly successful in managing your money, and can live and afford the life of your dreams.

This book is dedicated to all the men and women, who enrolled in my workshops, earnestly looking for ways to improve their financial situation. You have inspired me to keep learning and finding new ways (this book!) to help individuals navigate the confusing world of personal money management.

A big THANK YOU to all those who helped me with with this book. Your ideas and suggestions were instrumental in developing **The Money 20.**

And finally, thank you for taking the time to read this book. I sincerely hope that you walk away with some new ideas and strategies that will lead you to financial security.

SAVING AND INVESTING

"I'd like something that will make me
more attractive to money."

I am so confused about the stock market and choosing investments. I am in my mid-twenties and don't have a clue as to what I should do. What is the very best investment I can make?

The first thing many people think about when discussing investing and building wealth is the stock market. However, buying stocks is not the very best investment you can make. Do you know what is? Look in the mirror. It is investing in yourself!

INVESTING IN YOU means that you use your twenties and thirties to build your human capital, your financial literacy, your relationships, and your health. Use these early adult years to develop your goals and start making a game plan that points you in the right direction.

Your ability to create income is your human capital, and it is your greatest asset when you are young. How do you invest in your human capital? By taking advantage of every opportunity to develop additional skills, earn professional certifications, take training courses, and work in different areas that will broaden your professional horizons and increase your income potential. Become valuable to other people so that you can maximize your source of income. Remember, most people do not become wealthy by saving more; they become wealthy by maximizing their income.

You may be frustrated now because your income and financial capital are limited. You have debts, you have student loans, and you don't have much in savings or investment accounts. However, your human capital is immense. You have decades and decades to earn an income and build wealth. This is a huge advantage over the older generations. They don't have as much human capital left, their earning years are winding down, and they have to rely on the financial capital they have accumulated over the years.

Investing in your financial education is really important if you want to improve the quality of your life and your finances. Money management is a critical skill. You will be playing the money game your entire life, so learn the rules now.

Investing in yourself also includes thinking seriously about your goals and aspirations. What kind of life do you want to live? Where do you want to live? What are your values? If you just head off in any direction when you are in your twenties, you will end up somewhere, but it might not be where you wanted to go. This is the time to make a game plan and to start following that plan.

Invest in your relationships. Choose your friends carefully, because it has been said that you are the average of the five people with whom you spend the most time. So it becomes important to think about building a like-minded community of friends who will offer you support and encouragement.

Investing in your health is another way to invest in yourself. Developing healthy habits now is a very wise investment in your future. When I was in college, I took up running and walking. I lived in the city, and running around the park was a good way to escape the concrete jungle. I stayed with running through my early career days... and through my pregnancies, and toddlers, and on and on. A habit I developed in my early twenties has become part of my identity and has served me very well. If you can develop healthy eating, exercise, and lifestyle habits when you are young, you have a much greater chance of staying healthy as you age. This will save you a small fortune in health care expenses. Even now, as a young person, with the evolving healthcare landscape, more responsibility for medical expenses is being pushed from the employer to the employee. Many employers are moving to high-deductible health care plans. With a high-deductible plan, you are required to pay many of your health care expenses yourself, and then when you reach a specific threshold, the employer will pay for the rest. Medical expenses can be significant, and can quickly blow a hole in your budget and eat up your savings. Investing in your health when you are young is a very wise investment.

Do you know the two most common reasons people file for personal bankruptcy? Health care costs and divorce. Which leads me to my next point.

Marry wisely. You and your spouse will create the most important team of your life. You will want to make sure your team shares similar financial values so that you can work together toward common goals. And I won't even mention that a divorce is unbelievably costly and can derail the best financial plans.

Remember, YOU are your greatest asset. Use your twenties and thirties to invest in yourself so that you can generate the greatest returns for your future life.

I just graduated from college and received a $2000 check from my grandparents. I am one of the lucky ones, because I graduated with only a very small student loan, and no credit card debt. I already have money set aside for my apartment rent and security deposit. What is the smartest thing for me to do with their gift?

To graduate from college with only a small student loan and no credit card debt is quite an accomplishment. One of the most important steps you can take right now, to continue on a sound financial path, is to start putting money into an emergency fund. What is an EMERGENCY FUND? It is a savings account that can be used to get you through tough times. If you have an emergency fund, you can use that money to take care of major unexpected things that happen. And things do happen... that is reality. If you lose your job, lose your roommate, lose your car, or have a medical emergency, you will want to have money set aside that can carry you through. If there is no emergency fund, then you will have to rely on credit cards or personal loans. As you know, debt will reach in and steal your life right out from under you. And since you have been so careful to avoid debt, you want to continue your good track record.

As a young person starting out, aim for an emergency fund that can cover three months of basic living expenses. I know that sounds like a lot. It is. It will take time to build. But you have an excellent start with the gift from your grandparents. That will be your first deposit. If you have no other pressing expenses, deposit the entire check. Then set up an automatic deposit from your paycheck into the emergency fund. Set it up once and you won't have to think about it again. That is a key point, to automate the deposit each month. Once and done.

When you have three months of expenses set aside, pat yourself on your back. Having an emergency fund is really, really important! It will give you such a good feeling, knowing that you can handle financial setbacks. But don't stop there. Keep adding to it, until you have six months of basic expenses saved. This is not going to be easy, and it is going to take some time, but it is one of your most important financial goals. Did you know that the average American is only two paychecks away from a financial crisis? That is, if they were to miss their next two paychecks, they would be in BIG trouble. This cuts across most income levels. You do not want to handle your finances like everyone else. You can do better. Think about how financially secure you would feel if you had a three month or six month savings cushion.

Keep your emergency fund in a bank account that is not easily accessible. It would be better if it were not linked to your checking account. Why not link it? Because then it is a little too easy to dip into when you run short of money for your everyday expenses. This account is for the big emergency, such as a job loss or major car repair. This money does not belong in the stock market or other long-term investments. It should be in an account that is separate from any accounts you are using to save up for long-term purchases such as a vacation or house. A boring savings account or a money market account will be just fine.

Yes, I know the interest rates are almost non-existent for savings accounts. The purpose of your emergency fund is not to make money, it is to provide you with a cash cushion so you can avoid taking on credit card debt. From a growth perspective, avoiding paying interest on debt is just as powerful as generating returns on investments. Most importantly, an emergency fund provides peace of mind.

Congratulations on a very good start with your finances!

Finally, after searching for nine months, I just landed a good job! I have received all the information on our benefits, and they do offer a 401(k) retirement plan. Everyone is telling me that I should sign up as soon as I can for the 401(k). What do you think? And what investments should I select?

I don't care if your parents and your human resource contact, and your best friend are all telling you to enroll in your 401(k) plan at work. I don't care if you have seen the illustration that shows if you just contribute $2000 a year into your 401(k) from the ages of twenty-five to thirty-five, and never make any further contributions, through the power of compounding and deferred taxes, you will retire a millionaire.

The illustrations make it seem like a no-brainer, and that enrolling in the plan is the very first thing that you should on your very first day of work. Not really.

THE TRUTH IS, CONTRIBUTING TO A 401(k) IS NOT FOR EVERYONE

Let's back up a minute and explain these plans. A 401(k) is a retirement savings plan offered by employers so that you can save for retirement. You choose how much money you would like to save, and then that money is taken directly from your paycheck, before taxes, and placed into an account that belongs specifically to you. The money in this account will grow tax-deferred, and you will not pay taxes on this money until you start taking withdrawals at retirement. As an added bonus, the employer may also make contributions into your account.

Sounds like a pretty sweet deal... and it can be... but here are five good reasons NOT to enroll in your company's retirement plan:

1. You do not have an emergency fund. What is an emergency fund? It is a savings account that can be used to get you through tough times. An emergency fund will enable you to pay for major unexpected expenses, instead of putting them on a credit card. An emergency fund will cover your living expenses if you lose your job. An emergency fund is a safety net, and funding it should be one of your top financial priorities.

2. You have credit card debt. I hate credit card debt because it is like having a big, squishy leech sucking your hard-earned money right out of you. And, just like a leech hangs on really tightly, once you have taken on credit card debt, it is very hard to get rid of. Between exorbitant interest rates, over-limit fees, late payment penalties, and all the other blood-sucking fees, it can be very difficult to whittle down your balance. If you have credit card debt, it makes no sense to take some of your paycheck and put it in your 401(k) plan with the intention to have it grow, if at the same time, the interest on your credit card debt is growing twice as fast as the earnings in your retirement plan. **There is one important exception to this recommendation.** If your employer

matches your contributions to the 401(k) plan, then you really want to contribute and grab those matching dollars. So, if your employer does NOT match your contributions, then consider using the money were going to put in your retirement plan to pay off your credit card debt.

3. Your employer doesn't match contributions. One of the big benefits of a 401(k) comes from employer matches on contributions. If you are lucky, your employer will match your contributions up to a specified amount. This is free money. Free is good. Keep in mind that there may be a vesting schedule for those matches. What that means, is that any money your employer matches, may not be yours immediately. It may "vest" (become your money), over a number of years, with the maximum vesting period being six years. Your contributions to the plan from your paycheck are always 100% owned by you. It will just be the employer contributions that may not really belong to you until after a period of time. The good news, is that the employer contribution is vested immediately in about half of all plans. In other plans, you gain ownership of the employer contributions over time. For example, a four-year graded vesting schedule will give you 25% ownership of those contributions each year. This is an incentive to stay with your employer. Read your plan description, or ask someone in human resources for the details of your plan. If your employer does not make any contributions to your account, then you will want to consider other retirement savings

options, such as a traditional Individual Retirement Account (IRA) or Roth Individual Retirement Account (Roth IRA).

4. Lack of flexibility. When you invest money in a 401(k), you should not touch that money until retirement. If you need the savings prior to retirement, you may incur penalty fees and pay taxes on any withdrawals. Some plans do allow you to take out a loan, and those loans are not taxed, but they must be paid back. So consider that the money you are squirreling away will be for your life thirty or forty years down the road. That plan doesn't always work out so well, since currently, more than one out of four households either takes a loan, or an early withdrawal, from their company retirement plan. They all had the best intentions when they started saving in their plan, but life got in the way, and they needed to raid their retirement fund to keep them afloat. Just be aware that your 401(k) is not an emergency fund and offers little flexibility in getting to those savings.

5. High fees. There are a lot of fees associated with 401(k) plans. Some of them are paid by the employer and many are paid by the employee. Some plans have very low fees with index funds to choose from (which is good), and other plans have administrative fees paid by the employees and funds with very high fees (which is bad). When you are at the point where you are ready to start saving for retirement, you should ask a lot of questions about your

plan. If your plan offers funds with high fees, and if there is no company match, then you should consider an IRA or a Roth IRA.

As you can see, enrolling in an employer retirement plan is not a slam-dunk decision. Think about where you are financially. Do you have an emergency fund? Are you carrying credit card debt? Does your plan offer matching contributions? And finally, are you in the position to set this money aside and not touch it for many decades? If your current financial foundation is solid, that is, you have an emergency fund and minimal credit card debt, then a 401(k) plan with an employer match is an excellent tool to help you save for retirement.

I have about $200 each month to save OR invest OR pay off debt. What should I do first, pay off credit card debt, build an emergency fund, or save for retirement?

Excellent question! And considering that the average 20-something has a negative 2% savings rate - which means that they are spending more than they earn, usually financed through savings, Bank of Mom and Dad, or credit card debt - you are doing quite well to have a little extra money each month.

Your first two priorities should be to pay off your credit card debt and build an emergency fund. If you have credit card debt with very high interest rates, it makes a lot of sense to focus on paying off those debts as quickly as possible. However, it is also important to have an emergency fund so you won't have to rely on credit cards if you face a large unexpected expense. Perhaps split your extra funds between those two goals. Once you have at least $1000 in an emergency fund, then focus on credit card debt payoff.

When you have an emergency fund of three to six months basic living expenses, and your credit card debt is paid off, it is time to either save in your 401(k), especially if there is a match from your employer, or open a traditional Individual Retirement Account (IRA) or Roth Individual Retirement Account (Roth IRA).

I love Roth IRAs! They are a great way to save for retirement. If you are able to participate in a company 401(k) that has matching contributions, then you might want to fund that first (up to the match), and then save in a Roth IRA.

Unlike a 401(k) or a traditional IRA, you do not receive a tax break on the money you contribute to a Roth IRA. Roth contributions are made with AFTER-tax money. Traditional IRA and 401(k) contributions are made with BEFORE-tax money. It is somewhat confusing, but what that means, is that 401(k) contributions come out of your paycheck before Uncle Sam gets his cut. And with a traditional IRA, you usually receive a tax deduction. You might think that is very nice, to get the tax deduction right now when you need it. However, when you finally get to retirement, you will share all the money in your 401(k) or traditional IRA with Uncle Sam. Because he did not get his share up front (when you contributed, since they were before tax dollars), he now wants to share from your account. So you will pay income tax on every withdrawal you make during retirement.

With a Roth IRA, you fund the account with after-tax dollars, which is money from your paycheck, after Uncle Sam has taken his share. Since you have already paid taxes on those contributions, you do not have to share any of the account with Uncle Sam at retirement. All your withdrawals come out tax-free. This is especially valuable if you are in a higher tax bracket at retirement.

An additional benefit of a Roth IRA, is that if you face a real emergency (not just the need to escape to the Caribbean in the middle of January), you can withdraw your contributions (not the earnings), without any taxes or penalties. In the best of all worlds, you would never touch your Roth IRA until retirement, but sometimes life gets in the way.

In 2015 and 2016, you can contribute up to $5500 in a Roth IRA. There are income limitations with a Roth. If you are a very high earner, then you could be limited in the amount you are allowed to contribute. Generally, in 2016, if you are single and your adjusted gross income is under $117,000 then you should be able to make the full contribution. If your income is between $117,000 and $132,000 then you can make a partial contribution. For someone who is married, the adjusted gross income needs to be under $184,000 for the full contribution. Between $184,000 and $194,000 a partial contribution is allowed. I am sure you would love to have the problem of making too much money to be able to contribute to a Roth IRA! These figures are adjusted each year for inflation.

Keep in mind, that a Roth IRA is simply a savings vehicle. Once you open the account, you will need to make decisions on what type of investments you want to place in your Roth IRA. And this is where it gets really tricky! There are thousands of books and sites on investing. Everyone has an opinion. It will make your head spin.

You might want to look at the site, www.MoneyUnder30.com. It offers simple, honest information on both investing and personal finance. Or check out www.Investopedia.com which offers lots of educational tutorials.

My girlfriend and I are having an argument about saving money... so perhaps you can settle this disagreement. We both know that it is important to put aside some money each month; for emergencies, vacations, or perhaps for a condo down the road. But what we disagree on is just when we should put this money into our savings account. I think it should be at the beginning of the month, before we pay all our bills. My girlfriend says that makes no sense, we should wait until the end of the month, see how much we have left over, and then we can save that amount. Who is right?

Let me answer your question by telling you a true story.

I used to teach the Junior Achievement Program to middle school students. During the unit on personal money management, each group of students received a paycheck and a list of monthly expenses. One of the first questions I asked was, "When should you save money; at the beginning of the month when you receive your paycheck, or at the end of the month?" Every time I presented this program, the vast majority of students were adamant that they should wait until the end of the month so they could see how much they had left over, and that would be the amount they could save. And they were very strong in this belief. They would go on and on making their point. They would raise their voices and start jumping around at their desks (you know how middle school students can be).

Unfortunately, they were wrong. Because let's be honest here, we all have unlimited needs and desires, and IF WE WAIT UNTIL THE END OF THE MONTH, THERE WON'T BE ANY MONEY LEFT TO SAVE. That's just the way most of us are wired. I explained to them that if they followed the end of the month savings program, it was unlikely that they would ever build up a large savings account. We would then discuss how important it was to pay themselves first; each and every paycheck. They should be first in line for their money. Actually, Uncle Sam gets paid first. Your taxes come out before you even see your check. Uncle Sam is smart. If you received the full amount of your paycheck each and every month, and were then presented a bill from Uncle Sam at the end of the year for all the taxes you owed, how many of those bills could be paid? Not many, I am guessing. So get in line right after Uncle Sam. The government gets paid first, then you should pay yourself next, each and every paycheck.

How do you do that? The easiest way is to set up an automatic deposit from your paycheck into a savings or money market account. Set it up once and it will happen automatically, week after week, month after month. Paying yourself first and putting it on autopilot is a very, very smart financial decision. So you are right, your girlfriend is wrong. Enjoy it. This is one of the few times that will happen!

STUDENT LOANS

© Randy Glasbergen
glasbergen.com

"I've already forgotten most of the stuff
I learned in college. Can I just pay
for the parts I still remember?"

Y ou really, really wish you hadn't taken out so many student loans.

In your defense, it seemed a wise decision at the time. The economy was strong, college graduates were getting jobs, and a college degree was (and still is), the entrance requirement for many jobs. And you were stuck paying tuition and fees that have skyrocketed over the past fifteen years. The federal government was encouraging and backing student loans. The colleges saw that there was plenty of money available, so they kept jacking up their tuition and fees, knowing that the students would just keep taking out more and more student loans. This may be harsh, but it's the truth. You were stuck between a rock and a hard place. So you took out the loans that enabled you to stay in school, obtain your degree, maybe your graduate degree too, and get in the game.

Unfortunately, the game has changed. Jobs are not as plentiful for college graduates as they once were, and the pay is not what you imagined it would be. If you are one of the many 20-somethings struggling to find work suitable for a college graduate, you may wonder if it was really worth it to take on all that debt. Only time will tell. Your student loans may be overwhelming to you now, but who knows what the future holds? Ten years out, you may be using your education and degree in ways you can't even imagine now. It still holds true that the lifetime earnings of a college graduate are more than a million dollars higher than the earnings of a high school graduate. Your loans, although very burdensome at this point, may turn out to be a prudent investment.

Give yourself a break. You have your education and your degree (hopefully). No one can ever take that away from you. You were encouraged to take out those loans without really understanding the consequences. It was the job of the financial aid officer to help you stay in school. Period. Did anyone ever explain to you the monthly payment that you would be committing to by taking out these loans? Probably not. And were the loan amounts ever correlated back with what your potential income would be in your field of study, and if that income would be sufficient to cover those loans? Probably not.

Or perhaps you have recently graduated from an MBA program, or medical school, or some other graduate program, and your student loan debt is a really BIG number. Your income potential is high, and you would like to get out from under those loans as soon as possible so that you can have more discretionary income, buy a house, and start saving for financial independence or retirement.

Whatever your situation, your student loans have to be paid back. They are rarely discharged through bankruptcy. Overall, your goal is to get them paid off as quickly as possible, while minimizing the interest you pay over the course of the loan.

I am a recent graduate, with about $55,000 in student loans. The salary for my entry-level job in public relations is less than $30,000. I have started making payments on my loans, but they are killing me. After I pay my loans, rent, utilities, and buy groceries, I barely have any money left for clothes, incidentals, and going out with friends. What can I do to make these loan payments more manageable?

You are not alone in your struggle to pay off your student loans. Believe it or not, there is currently over one trillion dollars in outstanding student loans. Four in ten millennials say that they are overwhelmed by their debt, and much of that debt consists of student loans.

To give yourself a little more breathing room, see if there is anywhere in your monthly spending plan you can cut. Can you take in a roommate? Do you have a car you live without for a while? Is there any way you can bring in some additional income?

You have three other options:

1. Federal alternative repayment programs
2. Refinancing your loans
3. Student loan forgiveness

FEDERAL ALTERNATIVE REPAYMENT PROGRAMS

The government wants to be paid back, so they now offer a number of different repayment plans to give borrowers some flexibility.

Some of the more popular programs:

*   Graduated repayment: Progressively increases the monthly payment over ten years
*   Extended repayment: Extends your loan over twenty-five years
*   Income-based repayment: Payments are capped at 15% of your discretionary income. Complex program, need to qualify for it, remaining loan after twenty-five years will be forgiven
*   Pay as you earn: Caps monthly payments at 10% of discretionary income, payments last twenty years, payments change as income changes, and remaining balance after twenty years will be forgiven

There are many other repayment options. Check out www.studentaid.ed.gov for all the details.

There is also a repayment estimator at www.studentaid.ed.gov which will estimate how much you would pay monthly, and over the length of the loan for the various options. Start there and then be sure to contact your loan servicer for additional help. Keep in mind that if you extend your loan (in an effort to reduce your monthly payment), you will spend more in finance charges over the total life of the loan. If your financial situation changes, it is possible to change repayment plans, and you can do so once a year. Again, contact your loan servicer if you want to switch plans. As with all debt, paying it off sooner, rather than later, will reduce the total interest paid, and free up money to help you live the life you want. If your income increases, or you come into a financial windfall, consider making more frequent or larger payments.

REFINANCING STUDENT LOANS

A **Direct Consolidation Loan** allows you to consolidate (combine) multiple federal education loans into one loan. The result is a single monthly payment instead of multiple payments. The www.studentaid.ed.gov site covers the basics on consolidating federal loans.

There are several new, non-governmental options for refinancing student loans. SoFi and Common Bond (highlighted in the next question), are two options for high earners. One online service that has partnered with hundreds of local community banks and credit unions that want to enter the student loan marketplace is www.Lendkey.com. They help match borrowers with local lenders, and then facilitate the application process. Other major players in the student loan refinancing marketplace are Citizens

Financial Group, Darien Rowayton Bank, and Earnest. Keep in mind that when you refinance a federal loan into a private loan, there are some consumer protections that you will lose. These protections include access to federal income-based repayment options, public service forgiveness programs, as well as generous forbearance and deferral options.

STUDENT LOAN FORGIVENESS

Check to see if you are eligible for public service loan forgiveness. If you are a teacher, work in the government, military, or a nonprofit, you may be eligible for the Public Service Loan Forgiveness program. There are specific requirements for loan forgiveness, and it usually requires ten years of on time payments, but after the ten years, any outstanding balance may be forgiven. Again, all the information is available at www.studentaid.ed.gov. This may take a little research and some digging, but could be well worth the effort. If you are not eligible with your current job, then as you are considering your next career move, you may want to keep this in mind.

Each student loan situation is different. Do your research, shop rates, fees, and programs. You have so many more options now than just a couple years ago, and those options offer you the possibility of either extending the loans for a lower payment now, or refinancing, which could save you thousands of dollars over the life of your loan.

I am a dentist, just two years out of dental school, and have over $100,000 in federal student loans, with interest rates averaging about 7%. Is there a way to refinance these loans into a lower interest rate loan?

Historically, federal loan borrowers had few options to lower their interest rates. The federal government allows borrowers to consolidate their federal loans into one loan, but there usually isn't much of a difference in the interest rate. This is quickly changing.

SoFi and CommonBond are fast-growing upstarts that have emerged in response to the student loan crisis. They leverage the popularity of peer-to-peer lending, similar to Lending Club and Prosper, to give student borrowers a better deal. They offer both fixed-rate and variable-rate loans (for both federal and private loans), at much lower interest rates than what you are currently paying.

Both SoFi and CommonBond are looking for Henrys - High Earner, Not Yet Rich. They want college graduates that have good jobs, higher incomes, and good credit scores. They can offer these low-risk borrowers a better rate than the one-size-fits-all rates offered by the federal government. It makes perfect sense. Why should a graduate of Harvard Business School, with a six-figure income and excellent career prospects, pay the same interest rate as a student who took six years to get a degree in basket weaving? Similar to the way the interest rate on your auto loan, credit cards, and mortgage is based on your credit score, income and credit history, those same factors are taken into consideration on your student loans.

Some of the other major players in refinancing student loans are Citizens Financial Group, Darien Rowayton Bank, and Earnest.

Keep in mind that when you refinance a federal loan into a private loan, there are some consumer protections you will lose. These protections include access to federal income-based repayment options, public service forgiveness programs, as well as generous forbearance and deferral options.

If the loss of consumer protections is not important to you, then you should be able to refinance your student loans and save yourself a nice chunk of money.

What happens if I just stop making payments on my student loans?

If you stop making payments, you will be considered in default, and then a lot of bad things will happen. You lose eligibility for deferment, forbearance, and other repayment options.

The loan will be reported as delinquent to credit bureaus, which damages your credit rating. This will affect your ability to get a credit card, a phone, rent an apartment, and buy a car or a house. Your employer (at the request of the federal government), can withhold money from your pay, and your federal and state tax refunds may be withheld. Your student loan debt will increase because you will now be responsible for late fees, additional interest, court costs, collection costs, and on and on. It is not a pretty picture. You want to avoid defaulting on your loans.

Check out the www.studentaid.ed.gov site to get a lot more information on ways to avoid default. Except under some very limited circumstances, student loans are the one type of loan that cannot be discharged if you file for bankruptcy. So you are stuck with them. My best suggestion is to consider the various federal repayment programs and/or refinancing into a lower interest rate loan.

CREDIT CARDS

"And they lived happily ever after until the
credit card bills arrived and they realized
they couldn't afford to be quite so happy."

Let me just rant here for a few minutes (before I get to your questions).

DEBT IS A FOUR-LETTER WORD. Really. It is one of the nastiest of all the four-letter words. The thing is, you probably took on a lot of your debt when you were younger, in college, or just starting out. You took out the student loans, opened a credit card or two... or three, and now a few years later, you realize that the numbers add up quickly and you are drowning in debt. Or maybe not. Perhaps you just have a small student loan and some credit card debt, but it is still a problem. Life would just be so much easier if you didn't have those monthly payments.

You are not alone. Americans love to use their credit cards, and many carry significant balances. According to Federal Reserve statistics, the average US household that carries credit card debt has an outstanding total balance of $15,185. Let's go back a few years to show how this number has mushroomed. In 1990 the average cardholder debt was $2350. In 2000 it was $11,575, and in 2010 it was $15,624. It is kind of unbelievable how that number has grown. According to Federal Reserve statistics, the average college undergraduate has $3173 in credit card debt. The current 20-somethings and 30-somethings are really the first generation of students to graduate with a significant amount of credit card debt. You stepped on the debt treadmill very early in life. Don't panic, you have time on your side. With a plan and some effort, you will be able to dig yourself out of the debt hole.

There are many different types of debt. Mortgage debt, auto debt, student loans, home equity loans, medical loans, personal loans, and credit card debt. Sometimes it is prudent to take on debt. School loans (if not excessive), an auto loan, and a mortgage can all make sense at various points in your life. In this section, we are going to focus on credit card debt. Credit card debt carries the highest interest rates, most egregious penalties, and will sabotage your chances of becoming financially sound. It is almost impossible to be financially stable if you are carrying a lot of credit card debt.

The first thing to do is to stop beating yourself up over your credit card debt. Our culture encourages the use of debt. Don't have the money? Can't pay for it right now? No problem. Use credit. Our culture also encourages materialism and immediate gratification. Buy now: buy, buy, buy! No money, no problem, you can pay later. They sucked you in twice. Once on the front end, by encouraging you to buy more and more, and then on the back end, by paying later. It's a game and we all play it. But you are going to learn how to play the game better than many others. You are going to learn how to play to win.

The credit card companies market heavily to the young and impressionable. They want customers who will pay back the money they lend, but they really don't want you to pay it back too quickly.

Here's a true story: When my younger sister Patti was in college, she signed up for her first credit card and received a free coffee mug. She started using the card, received her monthly bills, and proceeded to toss the bills without paying them. Why did she think she didn't have to pay the bills? Because my sister, the business major, thought that you didn't have to start paying until you reached your credit limit! Ah yes, took her a while to dig out of that hole.

With interest rates as high as the mid-twenties (or low thirties), the credit card issuers can make a lot of money on interest payments. Add in late fees and over-limit fees, and you can see that this is a very lucrative industry for them, not you.

Here's an example - You purchase a new computer. It was on sale, and you were excited about that, but you didn't have much in your checking account, so you swiped a credit card. The computer was $1500 and you put it on a credit card that charges a 21% interest rate. If you only make minimum payments on this purchase (about $38 a month), it could take sixteen years to pay off that computer! Even more shocking, you would have paid $2,500 in interest in addition to the $1,500 purchase price. Your $1,500 purchase really cost you $4000! When you just make a small monthly payment, you don't realize how it all adds up over time, and how truly devastating minimum payments are to your financial well-being.

You gotta pay off those plastic weapons of financial destruction!

The only debt I have is four credit cards. On three of them, I have some pretty high balances. I want to get out of debt, but I am not sure the best way to approach this. What is the best way to pay off these credit cards?

The best strategy to pay off debt, is to FOCUS ON ONE DEBT AT A TIME. So which card do you start with? Financial experts have a long-running debate on this question. Some suggest that you pay off the highest interest rate credit card first, and then pay off the card with the next highest interest rate, and on down the line. Mathematically, that makes a lot of sense.

There are others who suggest you list your credit cards from the smallest balance to the largest, and start paying off the smallest debt first. You will pay slightly more in interest payments with this strategy, but a recent study by two marketing professors from Northwestern University showed that people who prioritized their debts from the smallest balance to the largest were more likely to actually eliminate credit card debt. You need some quick wins in order to keep you motivated and pumped up enough to stay with the program.

Everyone's situation is different. If you have a card that is over your credit limit, then that card should be at the top of your list. If you have a card that is charging a really, really high interest rate, then you could put that card at the top of list. In general though, I have seen people make the best progress when they list the cards from smallest balance owed to the largest.

Choose your first dragon to slay. You are going to put all your effort and any extra money you can find into paying off that first debt. Be sure to keep paying the minimum payments on all your other credit cards. Cut anywhere that is possible in your spending plan to come up with extra money to apply to debt #1. Be ruthless. When you have completely paid off that debt, you should reward yourself! You have made the first big step to becoming free of credit card debt. You will be proud, you will be excited, and you will be very motivated to take the money you were using to pay off debt #1 and roll it down to focusing on debt #2. You will now have both the money you were paying on debt #1 and the extra money you found to apply to this next debt.

Remember to keep paying the minimums on the other cards, and do not keep using those cards. Use your debit card or cold, hard cash. While you are paying off debt on the one hand, you do not want to be adding to your debt load at the same time.

The payoff strategy of focusing on one debt at a time works! I have received many, many letters and e-mails from individuals who have taken my "Living Debt Free" workshop, then went home and put the plan into action. They were thrilled! They made more progress than they ever thought possible with this simple plan. And once they start and see the results, they just keep going. It becomes addictive to see those balances decrease and then get blown away. They paid off their credit card debts, and they continued on to pay off car loans, student loans, and even their mortgages.

One online program that will create a personalized debt payoff program for you is www.ReadyForZero.com. You input all of your debts (credit card, car loan, student loans, and other loans), and then they will create your payoff plan and will track your progress. Very cool, very helpful.

Can you just imagine how awesome it would feel to have NO credit card debt, NO auto loans, and NO student loans? Think about that. You would have so many more choices available to you, perhaps a different job, different living situation, the ability to travel more, or focus on what you can do to help others. Being debt-free could change your life significantly.

I am sure that your next question is, "But I can barely make ends meet, where am I going to find extra money to put toward paying off my debt?"

Take a close look at all your spending categories, and think about where you can re-purpose some money for your debt payoff program. Are you contributing to a retirement plan that does not match contributions? If so, and you are carrying credit card debt, you might want to consider re-directing that money toward paying off your credit card balances.

In addition to changing up some of your spending, consider additional income opportunities, such as bonuses, overtime pay, part-time gigs, tax refunds, and cash gifts. Think about what unused items you could sell on eBay or Craigslist. Be creative.

Have some fun with your debt payoff program. Treat yourself to a special drink or treat when you go online to check your progress. Or, if you prefer, write your plan down on some really nice paper or a cool chart, keep it in a special, classy folder, or display the chart in a unique way. Have a favorite pen that you only use when you are working on your plan. You want to make this something you look forward to and feel good about. It is not a chore. It is about building a much better future for yourself. See yourself in that future where you are free of credit card debt. You are young and have time on your side. It can happen!

I have prioritized my debts, and I have a credit card with a really high rate (24%) that I am going to pay off first. A friend of mine suggested that I transfer that balance to a card that offers a lower interest rate, and then pay it off. How do I do that?

A balance transfer can be a really good option in your debt payoff program. Your goal will be to transfer the balance on that 24% credit card to a card that offers a 0% promotional rate for a period of time, hopefully at least a year. Then during that year, when you are paying 0% interest, you do everything you can to pay off that debt. Some balance transfer cards charge a fee to transfer your balance, which is usually between 3-5%. See if you can find a card with no balance transfer fee. If you can't, then you will have to take that fee into consideration when deciding which card to go with. Look for a card that offers the lowest transfer fees, along with the lowest interest rate (hopefully zero), during the longest introductory period.

One great site to help you compare balance transfer offers is www.magnifymoney.com. You enter your personal information, such as the amount of debt you want to transfer, your credit score range and the monthly amount that you can afford to put toward your debt. This site will then provide a list of potential offers and will highlight their rates, fees, and the fine print. This site can save you hours of research and aggravation.

When you receive your balance transfer card, don't put new purchases on this card, because the 0% interest rate may only apply to the balance you transferred, not new purchases. Some cards do offer a zero or a low interest rate for new purchases for a short period of time. This can be cumbersome to track. To keep things simple, use a different card for new purchases, or better yet, just use your debit card.

There are significant dangers to be aware of when doing a balance transfer. Watch for fine print that states that you have to pay down the amount of your balance transfer in full before a deadline to avoid paying interest. This kind of balance transfer deal can sting you with a year or more of accrued finance charges. Another potential danger when you cannot pay off the balance in full by the time the promotional period ends, is that you get stuck with a huge, double-digit interest rate on your remaining debt. You could try to transfer the debt to another low rate card right away, but if you are not approved for one, you could have to live with that high interest rate. Since you are already paying a very high interest rate on your current card, this is a reasonable risk to take. One late payment on a balance transfer card can send your rate immediately into the stratosphere. A balance transfer can certainly save you a lot of money in interest payments, but ONLY if you have carefully read and understand all the terms and conditions, and can play by the credit card's rules.

Remember, your credit score can be affected by closing existing credit card accounts. So instead of closing the old account with the zero balance, put that card aside, freeze it in a container of water, cut it in half, or do whatever it will take to prevent you from racking up more debt. If that card has an annual fee though, you might want to just go ahead and close it.

Another way to lower your interest rate is to use a peer-to-peer lender such as Lending Club or Prosper. These programs offer loans with fixed interest rates that can be 20-30% lower than most credit cards. If you have a job and a decent credit score, you make an online loan request. These loans are funded by investors, who would like to receive interest on their money that is higher than what banks are offering. There is a lot of interest in these peer-to-peer lenders and they are growing rapidly. They are approved in most, but not all states. They are a good alternative to help you lower your interest payments and move your debt payoff program forward.

I have several credit cards with very high interest rates. I would like to see if a peer-to-peer lender would approve me for a debt consolidation loan. Should I apply to Lending Club or Prosper?

Both Lending Club and Prosper are becoming very popular as online loan providers. They offer loans with fixed interest rates that can be 20-30% lower than credit cards. The loans are funded by individuals or institutions that are looking for investments that pay a decent rate of return. There is no downside to applying to both companies, because you can check the rate you qualify for without a mark on your credit report.

There are a few states that do not allow you to do business with Lending Club or Prosper, so the first step is to verify that they are approved in your state.

Both Lending Club and Prosper would like to see that you have handled credit responsibly, so they usually want to see at least two open accounts. Accounts considered are student loans, auto loans, mortgages, and credit cards.

Another factor that is evaluated is your debt to income ratio. Your debt includes your monthly debt payments such as rent or mortgage, credit cards, student loans, and car payments. Total everything up and divide by your monthly salary. The lower your ratio, the better. Anything over 50% is high, and it may be difficult to get a loan with either company.

Both companies advertise interest rates that are similar. The rate you actually get will depend on your credit score, your total debt load, the type of debt you carry, your payment history, income, and a few other criteria.

Both Lending Club and Prosper have excellent websites that explain their programs. You might also want to check out www.magnifymoney.com for other online lenders. This is a competitive business, so it pays to shop around.

Believe it or not, I don't have a credit card. How do I go about finding a good one?

There are several things to consider when shopping for a new credit card. My first criteria would be a card with no annual fee. Some credit cards waive the annual fee for the first year, but then stick it to you on an annual basis after that. I would avoid those cards, and narrow my search to cards with no annual fee.

If you don't have much of a credit history, or have a low credit score which is not uncommon for a young person without much credit history, then you may be limited to a secured credit card.

With a secured credit card, you make a security deposit of several hundred dollars, and that becomes your credit limit. A secured credit card functions in transactions the same way as a traditional, unsecured card. The cardholder receives statements and makes payments on the purchases. These payments are made with funds outside of those in the security deposit. Usually the funds in the security deposit are only used if the account has become severely delinquent. The fees with secured cards can be high, so do some online research to find a suitable secured card. Read the cardholder agreement very carefully so that you understand exactly how the card works. I know that no one really reads the agreements, but you are trying to build your credit, so you need to understand and follow the rules exactly. Your goal is to manage the secured card well, so that you can move on to a traditional credit card.

If you are a member of a credit union, consider their credit card. Credit unions usually offer credit cards with lower interest rates and fees. Hopefully, you will not carry a balance on your credit card, but just in case you get in a tight situation one month, it is better to pay a lower interest rate.

If you are not a member of a credit union, then check out www. credit.com, www.CreditKarma.com or www.cardratings.com. These sites sort credit card offers, based on the criteria you input. In reviewing the options, take a close look at the terms and conditions. Obviously you will want to choose a card with a lower interest rate. Keep in mind that the interest rate is variable, which means it can change at any time. The card company can increase the rate if interest rates rise, or if you manage your card poorly, which includes paying late or going over your credit limit.

Be aware that credit card companies can also increase your rate if you pay any other bill late. They will see you as a higher credit risk if you paid your cell phone bill late, and then they can raise the rate on your credit card, even if you have never made a late payment with that card!

Read the terms and conditions. You will be shocked at how high the interest rate can go if you are even one day late with your payment. Don't even apply for a credit card if you are unorganized in how you approach your finances and bill payments. The risks are just too high.

Finally, you might also consider the rewards offered, but at this point, that should be a lower priority. Know that the rewards are just a way to suck you in and encourage you to spend more than you should, and then the credit card companies are hoping that you pay late, or go over your credit limit. The rewards the credit card companies offer are just luring you into the game, and just like in Las Vegas, the odds are in their favor, and they are smiling as you make them very, very rich.

Applying online (through www.credit.com or one of the other sites), for a traditional credit card from Visa, Master Card, or Capital One is the easiest approach. You will need the basics such as your social security number, annual income, and you may be asked for information on the balances in your checking and savings account. You will receive either an e-mail or a snail mail letter notifying you if you have been approved. Then you should receive the card in a few weeks. If you have a low FICO score or no FICO score at all, your application may be rejected. Young adults are just starting to build a credit history, so it may take a few tries until you are approved.

I would encourage you to stay away from department store credit cards. They may be easier to obtain, but they contain several hidden dangers. First of all, their interest rates are sky high. Secondly, they just encourage you to shop and spend money. Yes, you might receive a store discount every time you spend, but if you ever end up with a balance that you can't pay off at the end of the month, the interest you pay will very quickly wipe out your savings discount. The stores know that if you are receiving a discount, you will find it easier to spend, spend, spend. Department stores practically beg you to sign up for their cards. Why do you think that is; because it is a good deal for them, or a good deal for you? I think you know the answer to that one!

"There is a magnetic strip on the back of every credit card. The magnets help stores pull you inside."

CREDIT SCORES

"I'm looking for an exorcist or a ghost-buster.
I'm being haunted by my past credit history!"

How do I get my credit report? And does the report include my actual credit score?

When you are applying for a car loan, a credit card, or a mortgage, lenders want to know the risk they are taking by lending you money. There are three major credit-reporting agencies that collect information on you and your financial habits. That information is then used to compute your credit report and your credit score. The most widely used credit score is called a FICO score. There are a number of other credit-scoring systems, but FICO is the score used by the vast majority of lenders.

Whether it is referred to as your FICO score or your credit score, it is a number that helps your creditors predict risk. It helps them determine that if they loan you money, or extend credit to you, how likely you are to pay them back in a timely manner. Your credit score is used to determine the interest rate you will pay on a credit card, car loan, or a mortgage. You may not know that it is also often used when you are renting an apartment, getting auto insurance, and changing cell phone plans. Many employers will also take a look at your credit report. As you can see, your credit history can affect many aspects of your personal and financial life.

The three credit-reporting agencies are Equifax, TransUnion, and Experian. They receive information from various creditors to build your report. That report is then used to determine your credit score. Your credit report contains many pages of information on all the accounts you have had over the years. It shows the average balances on your credit cards, your car loan amount, your student loans, and any other debt you may have now, or have had in the past. It shows if you have paid on time, and if not, how late you were in making payments. It will list any loans that you were not able to pay, and that were written off.

You are legally entitled to one free report from each of the agencies every year. You can get these free reports at the government site www.annualcreditreport.com. You should review your credit reports to make sure that they are accurate. It has been reported that more than 25% of reports have serious errors, so don't be surprised if you find information on your report that is not correct. You can file a dispute with the credit bureau (their site will explain how to go about challenging inaccurate information), but it can often be a long, difficult process to get the error corrected. Be persistent.

The credit reports from www.annualcreditreport.com do not contain your actual credit score. The score used to be a highly guarded secret, and you would have to go to www.myfico.com and pay $19.95 for your credit score.

Thankfully, things are changing quickly in the credit-scoring world. There are now several sites where you can get your credit score for free. At the top of the list is www.CreditKarma.com. They offer access to both your TransUnion, and Equifax, credit reports and credit scores. They also provide a Credit Report Card which assigns a grade to each of the main factors that go into your credit score. You will be able to see exactly which factor(s) is dragging down your score, and it will offer suggestions on the most effective ways to improve your credit score. They also offer credit monitoring for free. Other very helpful sites to check out are www.credit.com and www.CreditSesame.com. All of these sites offer a lot of useful information in understanding your credit report and score, but you may have to deal with product pitches for loans and follow-up marketing. Several credit card companies are now offering free credit scores for their customers, so you may be able to get your credit score directly from your credit card company.

I am going to be shopping for a car, and have been told that the interest rate I will pay is based on my credit score. How does that work? And how do they determine my score?

In the FICO system, the scores range from 300 to 850. Scores over 760 will usually get you the best interest rates on credit cards, auto loans, and mortgages. Someone with a score over 760 may receive an interest rate on an auto loan that is significantly less, as much as seven percentage points less, than someone with a score in the 500s. That higher interest rate will add up to thousands of dollars over the course of the loan. As you can see, your credit score is a very big deal!

There are five key inputs used in determining your credit score. Let's focus on those.

The most important factor in determining your score is your history of bill payments. Up to 35% of your FICO score is based on your payment history. If your payment for any bill is received even one day late, it will lower your score. You have a lot of control in this area. It is really important to pay all your bills on time, each and every month.

The second major input is your outstanding debt. This includes the total amount of debt you owe relative to your credit limits. If you have a credit limit on one of your credit cards of $3000 and you only owe $300 on that card, then your credit utilization on that card is low and that helps your credit score. However, if you have a card with a $3000 limit and you have a balance of $2500, you have a high credit utilization and it would lower your score. FICO has said that consumers with the best scores have a tendency to use only around 10% of the available credit on their credit cards. That is a low number. You really need to keep an eye on your balances. Since you will be shopping for a car loan soon, it would make sense to lower any outstanding credit card balances. Here's an additional tip - you don't know exactly when the credit agencies will be looking at your credit card balances. Will they be checking them early in the month, right after you have paid your monthly bill, or will they look at the end of the month, when your balance is higher? It is to your benefit to have a low credit utilization ratio, so pay off any balances as soon as you can, even before the due date.

The third input is your credit history. A 20-something will not have a very long track record in paying bills or using credit wisely, so their scores will typically be lower than the general population. There is not much you can do about this. It takes time to build up good credit. When it comes to credit cards, the longer an account is open, the better it is for your credit score. Therefore, it can hurt your score to close down a credit card that you have had for a long time. If you have a credit card that you no longer want, just cut up the card (or freeze it in a block of ice), but leave the account open. The exception to that would be if the account charges an annual fee.

The last two factors which help determine your score are the mix of credit (types of loans you have), and the number of new credit accounts that you have recently opened. Since you will soon be shopping for a car loan, you will want to avoid opening any new credit cards.

I recently checked my credit score, and was really disappointed that it was so low. What can I do to increase it?

According to the Experian credit bureau, the average credit score for millennials is 628, for Baby Boomers it is 700. It takes time, and a good credit history, to get that coveted high score. There are several things you can do to raise your score. It will take a while, but your efforts can really pay off in this area.

1. Pay your bills (all your bills) on time! Set up auto payments whenever possible to help prevent late payments due to bills getting lost in a pile of mail, or just getting overlooked. Even one late payment can drop your score by 100 points or more.

2. Maintain reasonable debt for your income level.

3. Avoid maxing out credit cards. Keep your credit utilization on each card as low as possible. Your credit utilization is the amount you owe on a card, relative to your credit limit. If possible, keep your utilization to 10% or less. I know that is not much, but that is how you earn the best credit scores. And the bad news, just one maxed out card can lower your score by up to 45 points.

4. If you have a credit card with a low limit, say only $500, and your balance is high, let's say $400, then that high utilization rate is having a much greater impact on your

score than loans with higher balances, for example, student loans. Pay off that credit card and you should see a nice increase in your credit score.

5. If you have self-discipline, and if you have a good payment history with a credit card issuer, you could ask to have your credit limit raised. That will help lower your utilization ratio. But DON'T use that increased limit as an excuse to spend more on that card.

6. Only apply for credit that you need. Do not open credit cards to take advantage of special discounts or promotions.

7. Don't open and close credit card accounts on a random basis. Every new card lowers your score, and closing established accounts also lowers your score.

SPENDING

"I found the problem. We earn money 5 days
a week, but we spend money 7 days a week."

Money will buy.....
A bed, but not sleep;
A book, but not brains;
Food, but not an appetite;
Medicine, but not health;
Luxuries, but not culture;
Amusement, but not
happiness.

-AUTHOR UNKNOWN

SMART SPENDING

You have limited resources. Your paycheck doesn't go as far as you would like. And you have values that are unique to you. Your values are the principles by which you live your life, and the aspects of your life that are of long-term importance to you. The next step is to match your limited money supply to your personal values. You want to make sure that you are using your money to buy the life that reflects your values. Doesn't that make perfect sense? It is like being a little kid again and walking into a wonderful candy store with a five-dollar bill gripped tightly in your fist. Everything in the store looks so tasty and inviting, but you only have five dollars, so you need to focus and buy only your very favorite treats.

If you spend your money in harmony with your deeply felt values, then you will be buying the life that you want, and that will bring you more happiness. Every spending decision you make is important. Unfortunately, most of the time we are on autopilot with our spending. We are just sort of going along and spending our money like our friends and co-workers spend their money. If we are at a certain income level, then we think we need to spend our money in ways that reflect that income level. To spend smart, we should be spending our money in ways that reflect our personal values.

What exactly are these values? Typical American values would include family life, spiritual life, health, romantic life, an engaging career, time for leisure, social activities, travel, and financial security. Some of these values will be more important to you than others. As you make day-to-day spending decisions, think about how your spending supports your personal values.

You have heard it said a million times, that money can't buy happiness. But that is really only partially true. Recent research on the science of spending shows that money, if spent in certain ways, can indeed buy happiness. Money spent on experiences, instead of things, buys more happiness. Money spent on "buying time" can bring additional happiness into your life. Helping other people, with your money, will put a smile on your face and add significantly to your happiness bucket.

Buying something now, and then waiting to enjoy it later, increases the happiness factor. Think about the dinner reservation you were able to snag for the best new sushi restaurant in town. You have to wait a month for the big day, but you will look forward to that dinner, and will receive happiness from both the anticipation *and* the dinner. Or when you pay for a vacation up front; you have months of enjoyment thinking about and planning your trip. The vacation itself will bring happiness, and then you have the fond memories afterward. Happiness multiplied.

Think about spending your money in ways that maximize your happiness and support your personal values. If one of your values is financial security, are you allocating resources to a savings account so that you will have a cushion to get you through difficult times? If you value travel, are you putting aside some of your income for future travel adventures? Really think about your goals; both short term and long term. Write them down. Now you have a plan and you are much more likely to be thoughtful in how you spend your money.

Do I really have to set up a budget?

No. You don't have to. The word "budget" has so many negative connotations. It tells you what you shouldn't do, what you can't do, and what you can't have. Who wants that?

However, you do need to know how much money is coming in each month, and how much is going out. And let's face it, money is not limitless, but our wants and needs are. So we need to create a plan which will help us prioritize our spending. We will call it a Spending Plan. That sounds better.

This is not about deprivation. It is about getting what you want with your limited resources. Your Spending Plan is the foundation upon which your entire financial life is built. Think of your financial life as a tree; an apple tree with a lot of fruit. Your Spending Plan is the trunk of the tree, rooted deep in the ground, giving support to all those branches which are loaded with red, shiny apples. The vacation you want is one apple. The car you want is another apple. The debt you want to pay off is yet another apple. The townhouse you would love to buy is an apple. Your retirement savings is an apple. If you don't care for and pay attention to the tree, then you won't get the apples. I know it is not exciting or sexy to focus on budgeting. Many books skip right over this topic and will coach you on how to find the next hot stock or mutual fund that will make you rich beyond your wildest dreams. That is a lot more fun to read about!

In the next few pages, we are going to focus on the trunk of the tree: your Spending Plan which is the foundation of your financial life. I am going to keep it very short and simple. Promise.

I am not a detail-oriented person, so where is the EASY BUTTON for figuring out my spending plan?

I get it. For most people, managing money isn't fun. It takes precious time, and it can be depressing and overwhelming. So let's figure out how to make this as painless as possible.

There are only three basic steps to creating a Spending Plan.

1. Know your monthly income
2. Determine your expenses
3. Manage expenses to reach your spending and saving goals.

That's it! Step1 is easy. It doesn't take long to determine your monthly take home pay. It is Step 2 and Step 3 that are much easier said than done. Tracking and managing expenses can get very confusing. There are so many categories, what goes where, how do you budget for an unexpected car repair bill, and on and on.

MONEY MANAGEMENT APPS TO THE RESCUE!
They link to your accounts, automatically track and categorize your spending, and help you to see, on a daily basis, where you are with your spending.

LEVEL MONEY is an app that is aimed squarely at millennials. It acts as a digital money meter that you can look at and see exactly how much cash you have to spend while still remaining in the black. Using algorithms and your financial accounts, Level Money figures out your income by looking at items like direct deposits of paychecks. Then it takes a look at your fixed, recurring expenses such as rent, cable, utilities, and debt payments. The difference between your income and fixed expenses, is your disposable income, which Level Money displays on a daily, weekly, or monthly basis. It updates automatically because it is linked to all your accounts. It also allows you to set up a targeted amount for saving, either for long-term or a specific one-time purchase.

Another excellent app is HOME BUDGET WITH SYNC. In addition to helping track your expenses, income, bills, and account balances, it offers support for budgeting. It also allows analysis of your expenses and income, including charts and graphs. It offers Family Sync, which allows a group of devices within the household (Android, iPhone, iPad), to exchange expense and income information, and work together within a single budget. Once it has been set up, the devices sync with each other automatically through the cloud.

MINT is one of the pioneers in personal money management software. Their app is very comprehensive, and offers expense tracking, bill reminders, auto pay, budgeting tips based on your spending patterns, and a big picture financial overview. Additionally, you can set spending limits for certain categories, and Mint will alert you when you are close to overspending. They also offer tons of online support.

There are many other excellent money management apps, so take a look at a variety of apps before you decide which one best meets your needs. Some of the apps are free, some are not. The best app is the one that makes sense to you, tracks spending the way you want to track it, and is the one you will actually use.

If you are more of a pen and paper person, there are hundreds of printable budgeting worksheets. You could check out "budget worksheet" on Pinterest and find many good options.

Although the money management apps can make tracking your spending much easier, it will take an investment of your time and energy up front. From choosing the best app for your situation, to inputting account information, to learning about all the features of the app, it will require some effort. But the payoff is huge. Can you just imagine how much better you would feel if you could cut through the money fog, and knew where your money was really going? And then by knowing, you could re-direct some of that money to spending that is actually important to you and brings you happiness. That's what it's all about. You. Creating happiness. Creating the life you want.

I know where I am spending my money each month, but that is not really a spending plan, it is just where it goes. What do I do next?

The next step is to take a closer look at each category. Are you surprised at some of the areas where you are spending more than you thought? Does your spending sync up with your priorities? Are you spending on things or life experiences? Behavioral research shows that experiences can have a much bigger impact on people's happiness than things. The choices you make in spending your money create your life. The science of smarter spending suggests that you can be happy at various income levels, if you use that income in ways that meet your specific needs and desires. In other words, don't follow the herd with your spending. Do what works for you.

After you have reviewed all your spending categories, the next step is to add another column that shows how much you would like to spend in that category. This becomes your SPENDING PLAN - how you wish to use your limited resources to create the best life possible for you at this point in time.

The final category for your spending plan is a dollar amount for savings. If you are in the negative each month, then you probably think that it is impossible for you to save money, but that is not true. Hopefully, you have found some spending categories where you can make adjustments; money that is either wasted, or not being spent in line with your values or goals. Rescue that money and re-allocate it to savings. There is one hard and fast rule in personal money management; You need to get to a point where you spend less than you earn. To get there, you have two choices, either increase your income, or decrease your expenses. Both are great options.

Your spending plan lays out the formula you will follow to get you from where you are, to where you want to be. If you are using an app, then you will be in constant contact with your plan. If you are a pen and paper person, then review your plan on a monthly basis. If monthly seems too much, pick two holidays, such as New Year's and the 4th of July to monitor and adjust your plan. Make changes as necessary. Track your progress. Hopefully, it will give you a sense of financial peace to know what you are spending, what challenges exist, and how you can achieve the financial goals that are important to you.

I am single, in my late twenties, and very healthy. What type of insurance do I really need?

I can give you some general guidelines, but there are always exceptions, and there are widely varying opinions on what types, and how much, insurance coverage to carry. So let this be your jumping-off point. Do your research, speak with knowledgeable insurance representatives, get quotes, and see what is available from your employer.

1. Health Insurance - YES. Your health is your greatest asset. You need to insure it, and you need to cover yourself in case you have an accident or major medical expenses. Since you are very healthy, you might want to consider a high-deductible health care plan with a Health Savings Account.

2. Auto Insurance - YES. This is a given, and in most states, a law. If possible, opt for a higher deductible so that your premiums will be lower.

3. Life Insurance - PROBABLY NOT. Since you are single, I am assuming that you have no children, and that no one else depends on your income. If that is the case, and there are no other extenuating circumstances, then you can probably forego a life insurance policy at this time. There is one very important extenuating circumstance, and it has to do with private student loans. If you currently have private student loans and pass away, your

parents (if they co-signed on those loans), will most likely be responsible for paying off your student debt. This is a situation that doesn't happen often, but it can be devastating for your parents. If you have private student loans, then you should strongly consider a life insurance policy to cover that responsibility.

4. Disability Insurance - MAYBE. IF you become disabled, who will care for you? Although you are single, will your parents step in to care for you, and do they have the resources to handle the needed care? Once you marry and have children, then disability insurance is even more important. Most employers offer disability insurance.

5. Renters Insurance - YES. It is inexpensive and protects your personal belongings from burglary, vandalism, fire, smoke, and water damage. Look for a "replacement value" policy which will pay the full cost to buy new furniture or electronics. If you live in an area that has earthquakes, you may need to purchase a separate insurance rider to be covered in case of earthquake damage.

6. Homeowners Insurance - YES. This is required for purchasing a home. Consider a higher deductible as a tradeoff for lower premiums. Again, if you live in an area that has earthquakes, you may need to purchase a separate insurance rider to be covered in case of earthquake damage.

Start your insurance shopping with your employer. See what they offer. Their group policies may offer very competitive rates. There are many online insurance quoting sites. A couple of the top ones are www.netquote.com, www.insureme.com, and www.einsurance.com.

I have heard of something called Bitcoin. What exactly is it, and how could it affect me?

Bitcoin is a digital currency (virtual money) that is quite interesting. It is a new technology that could change our current monetary system. Or it may totally flame out. It probably won't affect you at all in the near future, but over the years, it could significantly disrupt how our current financial system works.

I have a friend whose family goes all the way back to the Medici family of the Florentine Renaissance. The Medicis were the ones who figured out how to bring together savers and borrowers using the central ledger of a bank. They created a centralized system of trust to conduct business, and they inserted themselves as the middlemen. This was the start of modern day banking, which provided the engine for trade and commerce, that created the great wealth of many nations.

That same model of trust in a central banking system, using a middleman to conduct business, has expanded and flourished and is the current system we use in all our daily financial transactions.

What excites many, is that bitcoin offers a way to conduct our day-to-day financial transactions without the banking middlemen who skim a percentage off every single transaction. Bitcoin allows users to go peer-to-peer with purchases and cut out the middleman.

In addition to being a global, digital currency, the software supporting bitcoin offers a fundamentally new way of transacting and managing records online. There is the potential for the bitcoin architecture to disrupt not only finance, but other industries such as accounting and music.

The infrastructure that enables bitcoin transactions to occur is in place and is being used in many different ways. Apps are being built to facilitate the use of bitcoin, and venture capital money is flowing into this space.

Bitcoin is in its infancy. It was developed in 2009 and there have been, and will probably continue to be, many growing pains. If you find this intriguing and want to learn more, check out www.bitcoin.com or www.CoinDesk.com

ACTION PLAN

Congratulations on buying and reading this book! You have taken a really important first step in reaching out to learn more about managing your money.

You now have a lot more knowledge about money management. But guess what? Knowledge alone won't do it. You have to take action. Something. Anything. What do you think is the biggest roadblock to successful money management? Low income? Debt? Overspending? No, none of the above. The biggest roadblock to successfully managing your money is procrastination.

You are motivated and ready to start making some changes, but maybe you are a little overwhelmed. There are quite a few things to do that will improve your financial life. Where do you start?

CHOOSE ONE AREA, perhaps selecting a money app, OR figuring out which credit card to start paying off first, OR checking into refinancing student loans, OR setting up and making that first deposit into your emergency fund. Whatever you decide, do it within one week of finishing this book. Then when that step is taken care of, move on to your next "to do" item. Make a list, in writing, with a timeframe, and then check things off as you progress through the list.

You are young and by putting the effort in now, you will be building a strong money foundation that will serve you well into your thirties, forties and beyond. Your twenties are not a throwaway decade. You can't wait until you start making more money, or until you get that next job, or until you really get your act together before you start tackling money management. Start it now, working with what you have. Take the first step, and then the next, and then, little by little, you will start feeling in control of your money. It is an awesome feeling. You can get there!

Thank you for taking the time to read this book. I hope I have provided knowledge, resources, and motivation. I wish you much success!

RESOURCES

Saving and Investing

    Money Under 30   *www.moneyunder30.com*

    Investopedia   *www.investopedia.com*

Student Loans

    Federal Student Aid   *www.studentaid.ed.gov*

    LendKey   *www.lendkey.com*

    SoFi   *www.sofi.com*

    CommonBond   *www.commonbond.co*

Citizens Bank   *www.citizensbank.com/student-loans*

Darien Rowayton Bank   *www.student.drbank.com*

Earnest   *www.meetearnest.com*

Credit Cards

ReadyForZero   *www.readyforzero.com*

MagnifyMoney   *www.magnifymoney.com*

Lending Club   *www.lendingclub.com*

Prosper   *www.prosper.com*

Credit.com   *www.credit.com*

Credit Karma   *www.creditkarma.com*

CardRatings   *www.cardratings.com*

Credit Scores

Equifax   *www.equifax.com*

TransUnion   *www.transunion.com*

Experian	*www.experian.com*
Credit Sesame	*www.creditsesame.com*
Annual Credit Report	*www.annualcreditreport.com*

Spending

Level Money	*www.levelmoney.com*
Home Budget with Sync	*www.anishu.com*
Mint	*www.mint.com*
Pinterest	*www.pinterest.com*
NetQuote	*www.netquote.com*
InsureMe	*www.insureme.com*
EINSURANCE	*www.einsurance.com*
Bitcoin.com	*www.bitcoin.com*
CoinDesk	*www.coindesk.com*

FINANCIAL TERMS SIMPLIFIED

MONEY: A tool to shape your ideal life. Can be used wisely, totally ignored, or abused. Money has no power in and of itself. You exchange your time and energy to receive money which you then use to buy your life.

INCOME: Something that comes in, to cover what goes out. Your income may be low because you are early in the game. Your potential income over decades is immense.

WEALTH: A mindset, the ability to fully experience life, a feeling of abundance and contentment. Wealth is totally objective, and may or may not coincide with sums of money.

ASSET: Something useful or desirable, an item that has value, something that can be converted into cash or property that generates income. YOU are your greatest asset. YOUR human capital is immense. YOU have decades of earning power and potential ahead of you. Work on yourself, not just your job. Improve your skills, develop your talents.

LIABILITY: Owe to others. Includes required expenses to live, and your accumulated debt.

DEBT: Money you owe to others. Often, but not always, a four-letter word. Happened in your past, and steals from your future.

LIVING BEYOND YOUR MEANS: A one-way ticket to misery.

BUDGET: Outdated term. Replace with Spending Plan

SPENDING PLAN: Your choices in using your income to create your life. Without a plan, you will get somewhere, it just may not be where you really wanted to go.

FINANCIAL WELL-BEING: Your income minus your requirements. Simplify your wants, or increase your income, to improve your financial well-being.

Linda Schoenfeld is a CERTIFIED FINANCIAL PLANNER™ who specializes in financial education. She has taught workshops for thousands of baby boomers covering such topics as how to pay off debt, spend smart, and plan for retirement. She is also a retirement plan specialist, and has conducted numerous 401(k) enrollment meetings.

With two 20-something children, Linda is now focusing her efforts on helping a younger generation make good financial choices that will help them reduce their financial stress and enjoy a lifetime of financial peace and security.

Linda can be reached at linda.schoenfeld@gmail.com

Made in the USA
San Bernardino, CA
31 March 2016